Ouseburn Ancestors Publishing
6 Coldingham Gardens
Newcastle upon Tyne
NE5 3LS

www.ouseburnancestors.co.uk

ISBN 978-0-9927230-0-2

OUSEBURN FESTIVAL

All profits from this publication are donated to East End and Ouseburn Community Association, Registered Charity No. 1123860.

Colour Photography by David Lawson

Book Design by Colin Hagan at Northern Design

Printed by Alverton Press

GW00578357

Ouseburn Railway Viaduct after refurbishment, alongside
Byker Metro Bridge and Byker Road Bridge, 2013.

Contents

Preface

To celebrate the 135th anniversary of the opening of the New Glasshouse Bridge and Byker Road Bridge this short history of bridging the Ouseburn covers thirteen river crossings in the half-mile stretch of the Lower Ouseburn Valley from the Ouseburn Viaduct to the Low Level Bridge where the river enters the River Tyne.

As I gathered the information for this book it became apparent that the unique area of Ouseburn in east Newcastle upon Tyne is not only the cradle of the industrial revolution in the north-east of England but it is also home to some of the most innovative engineering in the history of bridge building, as well as charting the development of road and rail transport from its beginnings right up to 2013.

The valley was once steep-sided, and difficult to cross, which hampered both the growth and the transport links of Newcastle upon Tyne into the suburbs of Byker, Heaton and Walker.

The area has developed from arable land, before Roman Britain through the industrial revolution declining from the 1960s onwards, but it is now re-emerging as a cradle of art and creative industries while preserving its rich industrial heritage.

Acknowledgements

Colin Hagan of Northern Design
Dale Bolland and Ray Bland of The Ouseburn Trust
Jo Hodson of The Cumberland Arms
Mike Greathbatch
Newcastle City Library Local Studies and in particular Sarah Mulligan
Tina Webb
Alistair Swan, Chief Engineer, Newcastle City Council
Tyne & Wear Archives, Discovery Museum, Blandford House
Northumberland County Archives, Woodhorn Colliery Museum
Search Engine, National Railway Museum, York

Illustration Page 5 – Reproduced with permission of Tyne & Wear Archives
Illustration, Page 28 – Reproduced with permission of Northumberland Archives

A pier of Byker Metro Bridge stands over the original Bykerhill Lane route, 2013.
Opposite page: Cluny Footbridge looking west towards Ouseburn Farm with Byker Road Bridge, Byker Metro Bridge and Ouseburn Railway Viaduct, 2013.

Setting the scene

The Ouseburn river rises in the fields near Callerton to the north east of Newcastle upon Tyne and flows south eastwards through Woolsington Park, Gosforth Park and Jesmond Vale before reaching the Lower Ouseburn Valley where it joins the River Tyne at Newcastle upon Tyne's East Quayside.

Carboniferous coal measures formed over 300 million years were carved into by glacial erosion and deposition of shale and mudstone during the most recent ice-age leaving a wide and steeply-sided valley floor covered in lush green pasture on either side of the river. This landscape was developed as farmland and remained on the outskirts of Newcastle upon Tyne until the mid 1500s when it was annexed to the fledgling city.

As time passed the valley became populated with coal mining, the smoky factories of red and white lead, glassmaking, pottery and flax mills. Mixed in with this were glue factories and the cattle sanatorium. Road and rail transport then bridged the valley with associated industries of car repairers and scrap yards scattered about the landscape below these monumental bridges.

Today it is emerging once again as a centre for art and creative industries, a visitor destination with many live music venues. Businesses, residents, charities and volunteers are working tirelessly to ensure the future of the valley whilst nurturing its industrial past.

Stonyford

The first of the thirteen crossings of the lower valley occurred at the shallowest part of the river quite close to where the Cluny Slipway slopes down today. Here a natural ford could be used to cross the river by foot or with animals.

The first printed evidence for the existence of the ford is in the 1549 Act of Parliament annexing part of Edmund Lawson's Manor of Byker, to Newcastle upon Tyne. The description of the area to be annexed is mentioned in Welford's History of Gateshead and Newcastle:

'The uttermost part of the said ground and houses, at or on the river of Tyne upon the south, where a certain brook, or a little running water there, called the Swerle, cometh from the north, and runneth through the street of Sandgate into the aforesaid river of Tyne ; which brook or small stream of water was a division and separation of the said county and liberty of Newcastle from the manor of Byker, and from thence extendeth or leadeth along by the river of Tyne towards the east, nigh unto the said river of Tyne, stretching straight forward unto another small running stream, running also into the said river of Tyne, called Owes-burn, and so over the same brook of Owes, still by the bank adjoining to the aforesaid river of Tyne, to a certain other small water or swerle adjoining to the east side of the hedge or close commonly called St. Lawrence close, on the east side, and from thence passing northward by certain little hills, called Byker Hills, upwards over the said hills, towards the east by the space of 30 yards in breadth, and so along by the aforesaid hills by the aforesaid breadth towards the north, unto the south side of a certain ford called Stonyford, and from thence passing unto the north-east end of a certain close called Great St. Ann's close, adjoining to the king's street there, and from thence along by the hedge of the Great St. Ann's close southward unto the hedge of a certain close called Little St. Ann's close, and so along by the aforesaid hedge westward upon the south side of the hedges of certain closes called Durham close, Baxter's close, and Lumby [or Lumley] close, mutually adjoining to one another, unto the aforesaid little swerle or stream first mentioned, and from thence as the small swerle runneth towards the south through Sandgate, and so downwards into the river of Tyne in the same place where the first part of the bounds had its beginning." The said lands, etc., are to be incorporated, united, and knit to the town and county of Newcastle, and clearly exempted, separated, and divided, as well from the county of Northumberland as from the manor of Byker'.

In 1851 the ford is mentioned again in the description of the Census Enumeration District 2a of the civil parish of Byker. This natural, shallow river crossing would probably also have been chosen by the Roman surveyor to cross the Ouseburn during the building of Hadrian's Wall, a fact that might also have given the ford its name in later years as the wall fell into ruin.

A.D. 122

Roman Emperor Publius Aelius Hadrianus Buccellanus (better known to us as Hadrian) visited England between A.D.120 and A.D.122 and gave instructions to build Hadrian's Wall. From Segedunum (Wallsend) in the east, the wall was built mile-castle by mile-castle across the country to Bowness-on-Solway in the west. Mile-castle III was constructed at the west end of Stephen Street in Byker.

The wall here was narrow rather than broad and measured 8.3 to 8.8 Roman feet wide (about 2.5 metres) and was approximately 12 feet high (3.5 metres). From the Mile-castle at Stephen Street, the wall ran directly down hill to the bottom of the valley where it crossed the Ouseburn and ran straight up the other side of the valley in a line roughly matching Stepney Bank.

Crossing the Ouseburn at its shallowest point, the Romans would have constructed either a wooden bridge or a shallow culvert of ashlar stone, depending on the width and depth of the river at that time. (Ashlar is defined as a squared or finely dressed block of stone).

William Stuckley (1687 – 1765) was an early pioneer of archaeological and architectural drawing, as a way of preserving our historical heritage. His early travels around Britain in the 1700s were recorded in his work 'Itinerarium Curiosum' published in 1724. Included in this work is a lithograph or line drawing of Hadrian's Wall at Byker Hill, indicating that up to this time when he visited, the wall was mostly still intact.

As it was so long ago, by 1800 there were no remnants or evidence of the wall, but a mason working on building a steam-powered flour mill for Mr Beckington on the site of today's Ouseburn Farm placed three ashlar stones in the east quay wall of the Ouseburn, to mark the line of the wall as it crossed. To confirm this to be the correct line of the wall, a recent archaeological report, as part of a development for Tyne Housing on Foundry Lane, places the wall in line with this idea.

The location of this photograph showing the three stones in situ is at the north end of Foundry Lane and shows a pier of Byker Road Bridge on the top right, with an arch of the Ouseburn Railway Viaduct and Crawford's Buildings in the distance.

William Stuckley's drawing in his book 'Itinerarium Curiosum', 1724.

Right: 3 ashlar stones photographed in situ in front of a pier of Byker Road Bridge, with Crawford's Buildings in the background.

Opposite page: A drawing to accompany a proposed waggonway from Coxlodge and Kenton to the mouth of the Ouseburn, drawn on 6th March 1796, showing the 3 routes across the Ouseburn.

1600s

Footpaths and turnpike routes with wooden bridges

During this period the Ouseburn valley was slowly being transformed from farmland, and became littered with coal mining, and the beginnings of through roads for foot and animal transport appearing in clearly defined routes across the valley. The first wooden Glasshouse Bridge was on a riverside route along the north side of the River Tyne, and crossed the mouth of the Ouseburn. It was built around 1619 to allow pedestrians, and probably horses and other animals, to cross to the East Quayside where all of the glass-makers were located at that time. All of the plate-glass for windows in the whole of England were manufactured here, and then transported by sailing ships.

Sir Robert Mansell (1573 – 1656), a knight and vice-admiral of England in the reign of James I, established a glasshouse at St. Lawrence in 1614, using the expert labour of the Tyzack family who were Huguenot refugees originally living in Sussex. With easy access to the sea and a cheap supply of coal, Newcastle was the ideal place for Mansell's business, and by 1624 he was producing 6000 to 8000 tons of glass per year. It was James I who first prohibited the import of foreign glass and later Charles I granted sole license by Royal Proclamation to Mansell to manufacture window glass for the whole of England in 1635 at this site. Glassmaking continued on this site until 1759 establishing the name of this area of St. Lawrence, Byker as Glasshouse, although beyond this date most of the plate glass needed in England was still produced across Tyneside and Wearside.

The wooden Ouseburn Bridge was on the route to Shields, which became a Turnpike route. Turnpike roads began as early as 1663 and were privately sponsored, so tolls had to be paid by everyone who wanted to use them. There was a toll gate at Red Barns at the top of Stepney Bank, and another at Byker Bar at the top of Byker Bank. The Shields Turnpike road began in Newcastle and followed a route past the lower end of St. Ann's and down the hill roughly along a line with Cut Bank, and up the other side to Byker Bar. In early newspaper reports this bridge is referred to as Shields Road Bridge.

The third route to be established crossed the river at County Bridge (later renamed Crawford's Bridge) it ran from Red Barns, down the valley through Stepney Village and over the County Bridge. There it split into two routes, one leading back up to Byker on Bykerhill Lane, along a route now defined by Wilfrid Street, and another leading north along the Ouseburn Road route through Heaton.

These three early wooden bridges were soon replaced with single-arch stone structures to accommodate heavily-laden packhorses, carrying such items as coal down to the Ouseburn to be loaded onto sailing ships.

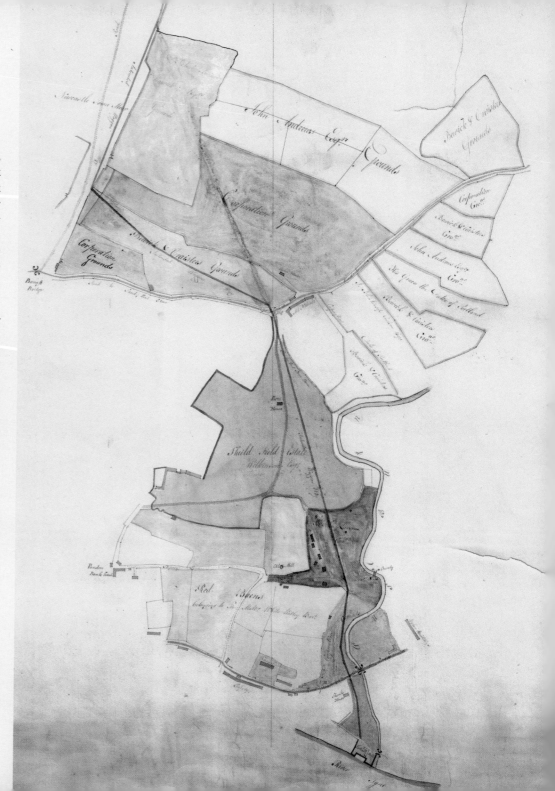

1700s

Crawford's Bridge

The stone structure of Crawford's Bridge stands beneath the towering Byker Road Bridge of 1878 and Ove Arup's 1982 Byker Metro Bridge. This is the earliest surviving bridge in the valley today.

On early municipal maps this bridge is called County Bridge as it stood on the outskirts of Newcastle and carried the route from Red Barns to Heaton over the county boundary into Northumberland. In 1750, John Richardson copied an earlier manuscript of Northumberland County rates. On the back page of the manuscript there is *'An Account of County Bridges in Northumberland'* written by Thomas Reed, Surveyor. The list includes a bridge called 'Ewsburn'. This information seems to suggest that Crawford's Bridge was built before 1750.

Eanus Mackenzie noted in 1827 that it was an *'ancient, narrow, and inconvenient bridge over the Ouseburn, a little above Mr Beckington's steam flour-mill, and upon the old road leading from Newcastle to Heaton: it is within the boundary of the county of Northumberland'.*

This single-arch stone bridge is a good example of the kind of bridge that stood on the other two original routes across the valley. They had low parapets which didn't interfere with the side bags carried by packhorses. Packhorses could be used singularly, but were more likely to be used in droves, one behind the other, with the front packhorse being called the 'bell-horse' as it wore a bell around its neck. This form of transport allowed great quantities of material such as coal or lead to be carried at once as each horse was capable of carrying approximately 128 kilos in weight, evenly distributed between two panniers on either side.

Crawford's Bridge also has large stones set just in front of the parapet walls which were probably put in place later to protect the bridge structure from cartwheels, as the horse-drawn carts turned onto or off the bridge. It is a Grade II listed structure, the listing describing the bridge as being built of coursed squared sandstone with a segmental arch. There are stone drains from the road surface protruding through the north-west and south-west faces into the river. An Ordnance Survey bench-mark is visible on the east parapet and a mason's mark of a diagonal cross in a square is etched into the west parapet.

Left: OS Benchmark.
Right: Mason's Mark.
Far left: Crawford's Bridge over a fast flowing Ouseburn River, 1962.
Opposite page: Crawford's Bridge, 2013.

Thomas Crawford was born in Callerton, a pitman until he was about 50 years of age, he became landlord of the Loraine Arms on the north side of the bridge in amongst some red-bricked terraced houses which he gradually purchased. They collectively became known as Crawford's Buildings. He died on 2nd September 1861 leaving his personal property valued at £300 to his wife, Rebecca Adamson Crawford. She became licensed victualler at the Loraine Arms, until she died on 26th April 1881, leaving only £50.

Such was Thomas' popularity in the local area that the County Bridge became known as Crawford's Bridge and this is the name that appears on Ordnance Survey maps today.

Old Glasshouse Bridge

This early photograph shows the original stone Glasshouse Bridge, built by Thomas Wrangham (1658 – 1700) a famous local shipbuilder in 1669, to replace the earlier wooden bridge thought to have been built in 1619.

The drawing below: Notice the 'Ship Tavern' in the background now known as 'The Tyne Bar'.
Facing page: Dismantling the Old Glasshouse Bridge in 1908.

John Sykes reported that on 2nd February 1777 *'Died, at the east end of Sandgate, Newcastle, Ann Forster, at the amazing age of 123. She retained her memory in wonderful perfection, until a few days before her death; had been supported only a few years by the parish, and the small contributions of individuals. In her early years, she assisted in carrying ballast from lighters in the river to Ballast Hills, now a public depository for the dead. She was born in the latter years of Oliver Cromwell's protectorship; and could remember the building of the bridge over the Ouseburn, at the Low Glass-houses, at which time she was about nine or ten years old.'*

This stone structure was altered in 1727 to make it level and 'more commodious' for pedestrians and horses. According to detailed photographs of the bridge during its demolition it was still just wide enough for a single packhorse or pedestrian to cross.

Ouseburn Bridge

In 1729 the wooden bridge on the Shields Turnpike road was replaced with another single-arch stone bridge called Ouseburn Bridge to carry the increasing amount of pedestrians and packhorses making the journey from Newcastle to Shields. This bridge was widened in 1790 to accommodate horse-drawn carriages and carts.

View of Ouseburn Bridge looking towards the River Tyne (Byker Bank is on the left).
Facing Page: 2013 view looking up-river (with Byker Bank on the right).

1800s

James & Co Bridge

James & Co built their Ouseburn Lead Works in 1801, on the west bank of the river just to the south of the area now called City Stadium. This is probably when another single arch stone bridge, very similar in size to Crawford's Bridge was built. At these works, James & Co manufactured white lead, which was used to make white paint. It was a very dangerous process, and mainly carried out by women.

The bridge is still in place today but has become part of the entrance to the culvert, sometimes known as Byker Cully. The James and Co Bridge was actually part of the leadworks site, and provided access to and from the west bank to the east quayside of the Ouseburn, and carried a road leading from the works to the north end of Crawford's Buildings.

The bridge can be clearly seen in the foreground of this photograph, which also shows Crawford's Buildings, and Crawford's Bridge is just visible beyond the terraced houses.

Notice the James & Co. Bridge in the foreground and the scrap-yard under the arches, a traditional business in the valley. The steam train is travelling east towards Newcastle upon Tyne.

Facing page: Today, the bridge is in great need of repair work to restore the parapets with a lot of the original stone in the river..

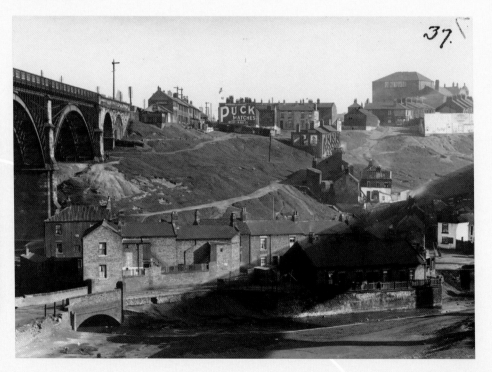

Ouseburn Railway Viaduct

With the development of railway as a means of transporting goods from 1825 onwards, the North Shields Railway Company commissioned the building of the line between Newcastle and North Shields. Ouseburn Railway Viaduct, designed by John and Benjamin Green was completed in 1837. John and Benjamin Green were also responsible for the designs of Grey's Monument, Penshaw Monument, and the Theatre Royal in Newcastle.

The original bridge was one of the earliest constructed with stone pillars mounted with a laminated wooden arch structure called the Wiebeking system. This pioneering system invented by Bavarian Karl Freidrick Wiebeking (1762 – 1842) in 1807, involved bending laminated wood into arched structures. His technique being unique in that it used laminated pieces of 12 inches thick.

The Ouseburn Railway Viaduct was built with five arches while at the same time the Willington Viaduct further to the east, which is similar in design, had seven arches. Benjamin Green, who was the son of the railway company's architect, John Green, wrote a paper on the Wiebeking technique for the British Association for the Advancement of Science in 1838.

As well as carrying the railway, the bridge had a walkway allowing pedestrians to cross from Newcastle to Byker and Heaton. Pedestrians paid a halfpenny toll to walk the perilous route to the other side and there are many newspaper reports of pedestrians being killed on the bridge. The viaduct also includes a skew-arch of ashlar stone over Stepney Road.

On the 21st June 1839 the whole country was celebrating the 24th anniversary of the end of the Napoleonic Wars in Europe. On this day the viaduct owners chose to hold their opening ceremony. A group of dignitaries gathered at Trafalgar Street Station to board two trains, pulled by an engine called 'Wellington', and another called 'Hotspur'. At 20 minutes to 12, the band of the Northumberland and Newcastle Yeomanry Cavalry played 'God Save the Queen' as the trains moved off slowly towards the viaduct. Crowds of people gathered along the route at every available view-point, waving handkerchiefs as the trains passed over the viaduct at 12 o'clock. At North Shields, a luncheon for approximately 800 people was held at the New Inn, Tynemouth.

Left: An early drawing of the viaduct taken from Jesmond Vale, with the Ouseburn Lead Works in the foreground and Stepney windmill on the right.

Above: The Ouseburn Culvert entrance is bottom left of this 1960 photograph. James & Co. Bridge is in the centre-right with Byker Road Bridge piers visible in the background. Crawford's Bridge is just visible to the left in front of Byker Road Bridge. The Ouseburn Railway Viaduct frames the photograph.

Facing page: The Ouseburn Railway Viaduct in 2013 after completion of renovation.

Proposed Ouseburn Road Bridge

In 1851 a prospectus was published by the Ouseburn Bridge Company calling for private sponsorship of a proposed road bridge across the valley from Red Barns in the west, to Byker Bar in the east. The proposal was to raise £12,000 in £10 shares for building the bridge. The committee suggested for the management included Robert Plummer (son of Matthew who was a partner in the Northumberland Flax Mill at 36 Lime Street), Stephen Lowrey, Henry Turner, Addison Langhorn Potter (who had purchased the Heaton Estate), George Cruddas and Joseph Grey.

It was proposed to build the bridge within 18 months. To illustrate to share holders the potential income generated from the new bridge, the proposal included a list of people and animals passing the toll collector's box at Red Barns in one week of December 1851:

43	Riding Horses
52	Carriage drawn by 1 Horse
22	Carriages drawn by 2 Horses
22	Wagons drawn by 2 Horses
1322	Carts drawn by 1 Horse
13	Carts drawn by 2 Horses
76	Cattle
408	Sheep
22	Pigs

According to this list of tolls, the amount of money that might be collected on the new bridge would have been £1,004. 18 shillings. The proposal also includes the statement that the Ouseburn Railway Viaduct was collecting approximately £150 per year at the rate of one halfpenny per person per crossing. This tells us that when calculated out in sterling

12 pennies in 1 shilling
20 shillings in 1 pound

2 x 12 x 20 x 150 = 72,000 people were using the railway viaduct to cross from Red Barns to Byker Bar or vise-versa each year, rather than walk down the hill and up the other side.

The proposal, included drawings by Newcastle Engineer Robert Nicholson (1808 – 1858), was deposited with Parliament, in order that an Act might be passed allowing the bridge to be built. However, on the death of one of the committee members, no progress was made on the building after commencement and the building work stopped.

1851 plan of a proposed bridge that was never built.

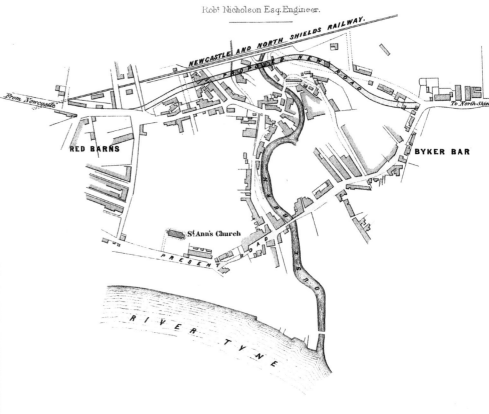

OUSEBURN BRIDGE AND APPROACHES.
1851.

Robt Nicholson Esq. Engineer.

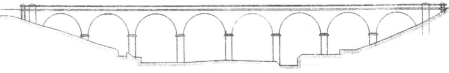

Elevation of Intended Bridge.

8 Arches, 58 Feet Span each.

REFERENCE.

The distance from the Red Barns to Byker Bar by the present Road is 1400 Yards.

Do   do   by the intended Road is   820   do.

Saving in distance by the New Road   580   do.

The Steepest rise upon the present Road is   1 in 9.

Do   do   intended Road is   1 in 20.

Ouseburn Railway Viaduct alterations

In 1869 the wooden arches of the original Ouseburn Railway Viaduct were replaced with iron and the bridge widened. This new iron superstructure closely resembled the original wooden design.

Notice the original stonework of 1837 contrasted against the brickwork of the 1869 extension.

New Glasshouse Bridge

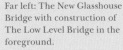

Far left: The New Glasshouse Bridge with construction of The Low Level Bridge in the foreground.

Top right: Two photographs showing The New Glasshouse Bridge with the Old Glasshouse Bridge in the foreground.

Bottom right: The New Glasshouse Bridge with The Low Level Bridge in the foreground.

Facing page: The Toffee Factory lighting illuminates the New Glasshouse Bridge in this 2013 photograph.

Means of transport moved on a stage further with the first cars being built in the 1860s and public transport in the form of horse-drawn trams commenced. In 1871 Newcastle Council Town Improvements Committee prepared a report on the construction of a new bridge linking the upper part of St. Ann's with the upper part of St. Lawrence but work on the resulting New Glasshouse Bridge at a cost of £14,000 did not start until 1877. The contract was awarded to Sir Walter Scott (1826 – 1910) and the bridge was completed and opened on 21st May 1878, five months before Byker Road Bridge.

Prior to the building of this new bridge, the only way to get to the upper part of St. Lawrence and then on to Walker was via Byker Bank, from the turnpike road which meant a half-mile round trip. This new bridge was built with contributions from property owners on either side of the bridge, on the understanding that the council would also build a new road leading to their estate in Walker, hoping that this would also lead to an increase in property values.

The opening ceremony included a luncheon at The Crown Hotel at the east end of the new bridge, a parade across the bridge accompanied by the Police Brass Band playing 'The Keel Row'. After a speech by the Mayor (Mr. Thomas Robinson) three cheers to the success of the bridge were given followed by the band playing 'The National Anthem'.

Taken in 1968, an Atlantian Double-deck bus crosses over Byker Road Bridge from Newcastle to Byker.
Opposite and next page: Plan of Byker Road Bridge submitted in 1871.

Byker Road Bridge

In 1871, twenty years after the first proposal for a road bridge over the Ouseburn, the subject was discussed again, this time by Newcastle Council. Plans were invited for a proposed bridge and a brick structure chosen, at the cost of £10,658 as brick would require the least maintenance. But, despite much council debate, the proposal did not go ahead.

The subject was shelved again, until a public meeting took place in 1873, with a resulting proposal to build a bridge costing £34,000. Again drawings were submitted to Parliament illustrating a bridge with a span of 1450 feet, comprising a 62 foot arch above the river, at a height of 106 feet, and a further 18 arches each of 60 feet wide. This plan was accepted although alterations were made which resulted in the finished bridge comprising of 14 spans of 60 feet and at the western end, eight spans of 25 feet. The bridge deck is 95 feet above the Ouseburn River and the original road deck was only 30 feet wide.

The work was given to Sir Walter Scott (builder) who was already engaged building the New Glasshouse Bridge, and had submitted a tender for the new bridge at £36,212. The foundations of the centre arches of the bridge were set in iron cylinders filled with stone and cement, as the ground in the valley floor was quite water-logged.

In 1877 it was decided to speed up the building of the bridge which resulted in Mr Scott instructing that all the arches of the bridge be built at the same time. This resulted in the bridge being completed by July 1878 enabling, after finishing touches, the first pedestrians to cross the bridge on 19th October 1878.

On the last day of 1894 Newcastle Council successfully bid to purchase the bridge from the Byker Bridge Company for the sum of £112,000. On the 12th April 1895 the bridge became toll-free.

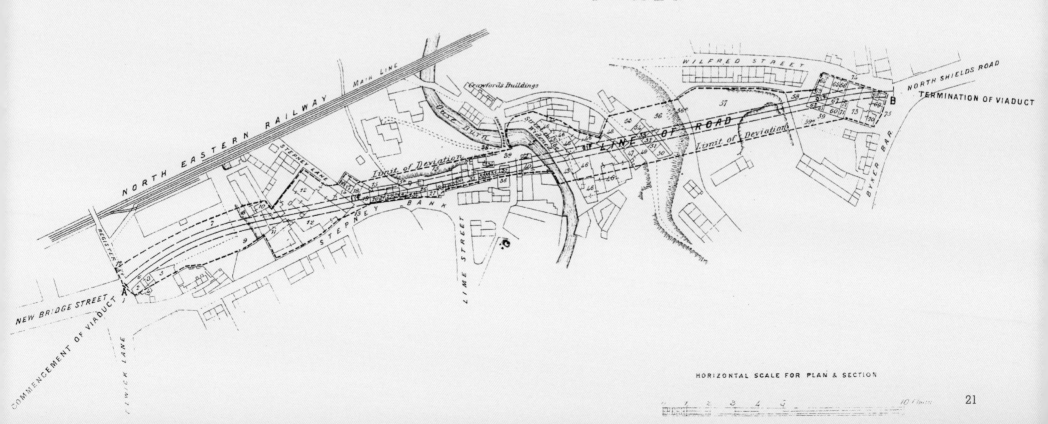

21

COMMENCEMENT OF VIADUCT AND JUNCTION WITH REGISTER STREET AND NEW BRIDGE STREET AT THE POINT **A** ON PLAN ON THE LEVEL THEREOF LEVEL UNALTERED

Stepney Lane level unaltered Height of Arch 35ft 0inches Span 60ft

Street level unaltered Height of Arch 88ft 0inches Span 62ft

Ouseburn Height of Arch 96ft 0inches Span 62ft Street to be widened level unaltered Height of Arch 95ft Span 60ft

Street level unaltered Height of Arch 65ft 0inches Span 60ft

JUNCTION WITH STREET ON THE LEVEL THEREOF LEVEL UNALTERED

TERMINATION OF VIADUCT AND JUNCTION WITH WILFRED STREET AT THE POINT **B** ON PLAN ON THT LEVEL THEREOF LEVEL UNALTERED

LINE CORRESPONDING TO FINISHED SURFACE OF ROADWAY

B R I D G E   4 5 0   Y A R D S

18 Arches of 60 ft Span
1 Arch of 62 ft Span

8.6

42.6

95.6
112'.0"
105'.0"

73'.6"

13'.0

21.6

RATE OF INCLINATION ONE IN 70

119.30ft
118.00ft

H O R I Z O N T A L

118.00ft

RATE OF INCLINATION

ONE IN 59

126.90ft

High Water of Ordinary Spring Tides

1 F   2 F   3 F   TOTAL 1

The DATUM LEVEL of this Section is 20 feet 10 inches below a mark cut thus ⚊ upon the parapet of a Bridge over the Ouseburn commonly called the County Bridge

Caption here

The Cluny Footbridge in the foreground with Byker Road Bridge, Byker Metro Bridge and Ouseburn Railway Viaduct, 2013.

1900s

Byker Road Bridge widening

Almost immediately after completion of the purchase of Byker Road Bridge, Newcastle Council set about planning to widen the bridge with the intention of providing a double line of tram tracks, ready for a new electric tram system. However, Parliament did not accept their proposal until late 1899. The plan to widen the bridge included the widening of footpaths on both sides, and the replacement of the brick parapets with lattice-type iron, with teak handrails.

The bridge widening of 10 feet either side was achieved by inserting steel cross-beams in brick tunnels at intervals across the length of the bridge. The work was given to W & J Lant and began in April 1901. Completion was in August 1902 at a cost of £22,280.

Notice the steam-powered crane and wooden wheelbarrows in this 1902 photograph on Byker Road Bridge.
Opposite page: Two 1908 photographs showing construction of the quayside extension and the Low Level Bridge.
Opposite page: Plans of Low Level Bridge from 1908.

Low Level Bridge

In 1908 the old stone Glasshouse Bridge was demolished to make way for a new dual purpose bridge which would connect the Newcastle Quayside with a new quay on the site we call Spiller's Quay today. The detailed photographs of the old bridge were taken during demolition, and clearly document the dilapidated state of the structure, as well as glimpses of the surrounding properties and landscape.

The replacement bridge was constructed to carry a road and a rail track, as well as water and gas pipes to the newly constructed east quayside and was made of iron plating held together with rivets. The plan shows that the deck of the Low Level Bridge was constructed using a method called 'Hobson's Patent Troughing'. George Andrew Hobson (1854 – 1917) was the Staff Engineer employed by J.W. Willans who was the main contractor on the Liverpool Overhead Railway (LOR) or more affectionately 'The Docker's Umbrella' designed by Sir Douglas Fox (1840 – 1921).

The structure of the LOR was 16 feet above ground level and approximately 5 miles long and required a strong, water-tight decking system to protect everything underneath it from water, oil and dirt from the locomotives.

Hobson designed and patented the Arched-Plate System and the Diagonal-Plate System specifically for the LOR structure in 1889, and following completion in 1893, the methods were extensively discussed in engineering circles and used on other bridges world-wide.

Perhaps the fact that the Low Level Bridge in Ouseburn was to be part of another dock railway system and is built on a slight diagonal led the designers to choose this new and innovative method of bridge decking.

Following completion of the LOR, Hobson went on to become a partner in the firm of Sir Douglas Fox and is accredited with designing the Victoria Falls Bridge over the Zambezi River connecting Zimbabwe to Zambia in Southern Africa.

Riveting

Riveting the decking and plates of the Low Level Bridge would probably have been done by mechanical means, but early, hot-riveting was the method used to join two sheets of metal such as in shipbuilding before the invention of welding during World War II. It was a skilled job in shipbuilding, carried out by teams of four men or boys, who worked in perilous conditions constantly in danger of burning themselves on the extremely hot metal. The team was made up of:

- Heater boy who fired up a small brazier and used foot-bellows to keep the brazier hot while he placed a rivet in the heat with long tongs until it was red hot. Then he was use the long tongs to toss the rivet up to a

- Catch Boy who would use a small wooden bowl to catch the red hot rivet. He would then use a pair of tongs to place the rivet into a pre-formed hole in two metal plates to be joined together.

- The Holder-up then had to place a heavy hammer over the head of the rivet and hold it in place while

- The Basher on the other side of the plate to the rivet head was waiting to beat the rivet down into place to fill the rivet hole and form a head on the opposite side. As the rivet cooled it shrank hard against the metal plates sealing the joint. These teams of four could hammer in 2000 rivets a day in the shipyards.

The Low Level Bridge on Quayside Road at the mouth of the Ouseburn has a special place in our industrial heritage as it provides a close-up example of dying skills and techniques used historically both in shipbuilding, and in boiler and bridge building, which have been replaced by welding technology today.

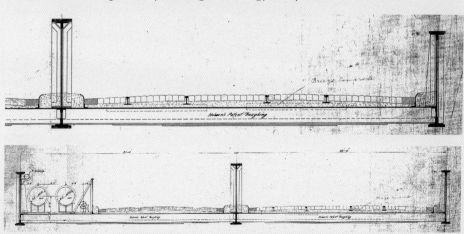

The Ouseburn Culvert

The idea to enclose the Ouseburn River beyond Jesmond Vale came about in 1901 when it was first discussed at the Newcastle Town Improvements Committee. The plan was to enclose the Ouseburn River in a concrete tunnel, in order that the council could solve their waste-disposal problem temporarily by providing the Ouseburn Valley below Jesmond Vale as a tipping site.

All kinds of domestic waste, coal etc. could be disposed of, while in the long-term new land for could be created for housing. The scheme would also provide much-needed access to the eastern suburbs of the ever expanding city.

The scheme involved the compulsory purchase of land and excavation work, from Jesmond Vale to the area just under the Ouseburn Railway Viaduct. A mill-race was constructed to re-route the river during construction of the culvert. Once completed, the river was redirected through the culvert under a concrete floor built inside.

The whole project was estimated to cost £160,766 and the power to proceed with the work was given in a Parliamentary Bill in 1904.

Again, a pioneering technique was used in the construction of the culvert. The Hennebique System of ferro-concrete construction was chosen by Newcastle City Engineers. This technique had already been used in the construction of the Co-operative Wholesale Society building, now known as Malmaison Hotel on Newcastle Quayside in 1902, and would also be used to build the Spanish City Dome in Whitley Bay in 1910.

The work on the Ouseburn Culvert was contracted to W.T. Weir of Howdon and this part of the whole project was estimated at £81,463. Francois Hennebique (1842 – 1921) was a French self-educated builder who pioneered and patented his reinforced concrete system in 1892.

W.T. Weir commenced work on the site in February 1906. During the course of construction 850 tons of steel and 17,000 cubic yards of concrete were used on what was the most important civil engineering contract on the north east coast at that time. The construction was completed in December 1907.

The concrete culvert is only 8 inches thick at the crown but holds 2.5 million cubic yards of material 90 Feet below the surface of City Stadium. In 1939 the culvert was converted to provide an air-raid shelter for the surrounding population with facilities for 500 people. The shelter had an entrance under the Ouseburn Railway Viaduct and another at Warwick Street. Inside the shelter there were offices for wardens, a canteen, a youth club, a religious space for worship, seating, bunk beds, a stage area for musical performances and a hospital room all fully fitted out with furnishings and accommodated on a concrete floor installed above the river bed. In 1941 a 100 feet crack appeared in the original structure of the culvert which caused the council to close part of the shelter. The remaining part was still used during World War II and in 1943 a Library and Reading Room were added.

Today the culvert is not accessible to the public.

Opposite page: Low Level Bridge with New Glasshouse Bridge in the background. Notice the wooden framework for the reinforced-concrete tunnel and how wide the valley floor was before enclosure.

Next page: A plan from the Ouseburn Valley Works showing the buildings and streets reclaimed when the culvert was constructed.

CITY AND COUNTY OF NEWCASTLE upon TYNE

NEWCASTLE upon TYNE CORPORATI

OUSEBURN VALLEY WORKS.
WORKS Nos. 1, 2, 3 & 4.
SHEET No. 29.

PARISH OF HEATON

PARISH C
BYKER

Ouseburn Lead Works

WORK No. 1

CENTRE OF STREET AND LINE OF SECTION

WORK No. 4

CENTRE OF CULVERT AND LINE OF SECTION

WORK No. 3

CENTRE OF STREET AND LINE OF SECTION

WORK No. 2

CENTRE OF STREET AND LINE OF SECTION

Commencement of Work No. 4 and Junction with the Ouseburn on the level of the bed thereof.

Termination of Work No. 2 and Junction with Newington Road on the level thereof.

Termination of Work No. 4 and Junction with the Ouseburn on the level of the bed thereof.

Termination of Work No. 2 and Junction with Newington Road on the level thereof.

Termination of Work No. 1 and Junction with the Newington Road on the level thereof.

Commencement of Work No. 1 and Junction with Dinsdale Road on the level thereof.

Limit of Deviation Work No. 4

Limit of Deviation Work No. 4

Limit of Deviation Work No. 1

Limit of Deviation Work No. 2

Limit of Deviation Work No. 3

LIMIT OF LAND TO BE ACQUIRED

STRATFORD ROAD

STRATFORD GROVE WEST

OUSEBURN ROAD

WARWICK STREET

HOTSPUR STREET

MOWBRAY STREET

BOLINGBROKE STREET

MALCOLM STREET

SOUTH VIEW

NEWINGTON ROAD

NORTH EASTERN RAILWAY

Parish Boundary

AMBLE GROVE

CHELMSFORD GROVE

GOLDSPINK LANE

BURNVILLE ROAD

DINSDALE ROAD

STARBECK AVENUE

MORRISON STREET

MARSHALL STREET

BRYSON TERRACE

STEPNEY ROAD

SHIELDFIELD ROAD

BERMONDSEY STREET EAST

SCHOOL

ASMOND VALE HOUSE

Ouseburn Bridge replacement

In 1959 the Ouseburn Bridge on the old turnpike route between Cut Bank and Byker Bank was dismantled and replaced with a concrete structure designed by Newcastle City Council. The new structure is 'fit for purpose' but visually has no place amongst the engineering masterpieces spanning the Ouseburn Valley today.

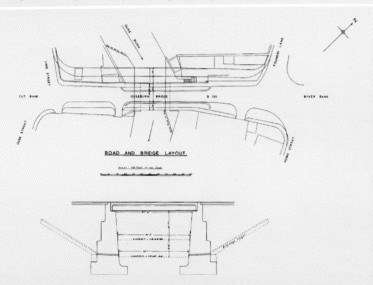

ROAD AND BRIDGE LAYOUT

Ordnance Survey verification of Bench Marks

Thousands of benchmarks were placed on semi-permanent structures like roads, boundaries and buildings, by Ordnance Survey, and used with a network of approximately 190 Triangulation (or Trig) points across Great Britain to measure height and distance during the 'Principal Triangulation of Great Britain' between 1783 and 1853. The process was used to draw the first accurate 1-inch scale maps of Great Britain which was completed in 1870.

In 1962, Ordnance Survey carried out a second triangulation survey and verified many of the benchmarks already in place.

The Ouseburn Valley bridges hold seven of these benchmarks. However, with the advent of the Global Positioning System (GPS) there is no longer a need for these benchmarks. This chart shows the Ordnance Survey notation and location of each benchmark on bridges in the valley:

As time passes, they will still be visible as long as the Ouseburn bridges are standing, but their significance in Ordnance Survey history may be lost.

Square	Easting	Northing	Mark type	Description	Height	Order	Datum	Verified year	Levelling year	Metres above ground
NZ	2600	6459	Cut Mark	Wall NW side Byker Bridge 1.2m NE fence and wall junction	34.7167	3	N	1962	0	0.4
NZ	2623	6466	Cut Mark	Br para E side Ouseburn Rd Str C	6.2393	3	N	1962	0	0.4
NZ	2632	6438	Rivet	NMB Rivet NE Br butt SE side road NE side Ouseburn	7.937	3	N	1962	0	0
NZ	2633	6482	Cut Mark	NBM Rly BR South View West W Butt	33.2202	3	N	1962	0	0.7
NZ	2640	6420	Rivet	Rivet N para Glasshouse Br prodn E face bldg	15.75	3	N	1962	0	1.2
NZ	2645	6416	Cut Mark	NMB NE para Low Level Br SE end	6.4831	3	N	1962	0	0.4
NZ	2676	6448	Cut Mark	NBM Rly para SW side Rd 3.0m E ang	35.7	3	N	1962	0	0.5

Byker Road Bridge strengthening

In 1986 Newcastle City Council completed an extensive project to strengthen Byker Road Bridge and resurface the road-deck to accommodate ever increasing road traffic. Today it carries the B1312 road and is a major route for commercial, private and public transport.

2000 and beyond

Byker Metro Bridge

The Byker Metro Bridge was a huge engineering work on a scale not scene in Ouseburn since the building of Byker Road Bridge in 1878. Another innovative engineering technique involving pre-fabricated concrete joined together with epoxy-resin. It was part of the largest urban transport system in the UK at the time which carried approximately 60,000 passengers in its first year of operation. The Metro was opening in the summer of 1981 by Her Majesty The Queen.

Ove Nyquist Arup, who founded Ove Arup & Partners was born in Newcastle upon Tyne in 1895 but his connection with the Ouseburn goes much further back than 1980. Ove was born on 16th April 1895 at 16 Jesmond Vale Terrace. The house still stands today on Heaton Road opposite the entrance to Heaton Park. He was the son of Jens Simon Johannes Arup and his second wife Mathilde Boletter Nyquist who had been governess to Jens' three daughters from his first marriage.

Jens Arup was employed as Danish Veterinary Consul at the time of Ove's birth and was involved in overseeing live animal imports to Newcastle, so would undoubtedly have worked in the Ouseburn Valley, at the Cattle Sanatorium. As live cattle imports were banned in the late 1890s, Jens moved his family back to Denmark but Ove's connection with the North East reappeared with the formation of his business in the 1940s.

Ove's life-long passion was to promote what he called 'total architecture' a marriage of engineering and architecture throughout a building project. He famously engineered the Sydney Opera House, Centre Pompidou in Paris, Highpoint 1 in London, Coventry Cathedral and Kingsgate Bridge in Durham in 1963.

Kingsgate Bridge was reputed to be his favourite work, and in 1988 he had his ashes scattered into the river Wear from the centre of the bridge. In 1974 his company designed the 'S'- shaped masterpiece known as Byker Metro Bridge. Towering 30 metres above the Ouseburn the bridge was the first in Britain to be built using cantilevered concrete sections with epoxy-resin glued joints.

Each of the arches is approximately 68.9 metres long, one of them standing over a footpath on the original Bykerhill Lane route up to Byker Bar.

Byker Metro Bridge stands in front of the Ouseburn Railway Viaduct with Crawford's Bridge in the foreground.

The Cluny Footbridge

The Cluny Footbridge was put into place in 2004 when the Eco Centre was built on the site of Byker Farm which had been closed several years previously, due to contamination in the land. The bridge was designed, built and installed by Concrete and Timber Services Limited to replace an earlier footbridge built by The Territorial Army.

The bridge is 3 metres wide and has a span of 9 metres. When the tide in the River Tyne is out, the level of the water can be very low almost replicating the natural ford that once occurred here, but the bridge is normally about 2 metres above the water level. Before the Territorial Army's Bridge was put in place, the only way to cross the Ouseburn River at this point was on foot, wading across the water and negotiating the cobbled lane up towards what is now Village Green.

The Cluny Footbridge, 2013.
Far right: Detail views of the Ouseburn Railway Viaduct refurbishment, 2013.

Ouseburn Railway Viaduct Renovation

The renovation of the Ouseburn Railway Viaduct started in 2012 and was completed in March 2013. For over a year the bridge was hidden from view, wrapped in a white polythene coat over scaffolding to shield the valley from contamination and the bridge from the elements, while Carillion carried out extensive structural repairs and repainting. The renovation, in consultation with English Heritage, involved the strengthening of the original structure, whilst maintaining, as far as possible, the outer appearance of the original structure.

The renovation included the use of another innovative process in bridge maintenance, of coating the superstructure with a new paint product called M20 RT98 System. This paint system was developed by another north east company established in 1973. Pyeroy was established by Bob Thompson in Felling to pioneer protective coatings for shipbuilding and later civil engineering.

The company had already re-painted the Swing Bridge over the River Tyne (1868-1876) in 1985 as well as painting the QEII Metro Bridge, the High Level Bridge and the Tyne Bridge. Nationally they had also repainted Tower Bridge, Southwark and Blackfriar's Bridges in London and Forth Rail Bridge in Edinburgh. The M20 RT98 paint system is expected to last for 25 years or more.

In March 2013 the white polythene coat was removed from the Ouseburn Railway Viaduct to reveal a new coating of deep grey paint contrasting against the stone structure beneath the railway.

Byker Road Bridge refurbishment

During 2012/13 approximately £100,000 was spent re-pointing large sections of the brickwork and refurbishing the drainage system on Byker Road Bridge. The work was carried out by Colas (N) Ltd and involved using high-reach platforms and abseiling techniques to complete the work.

The future of these structures across the Ouseburn

Demonstrating almost 400 years of civil engineering history in road and bridge-building techniques the bridging of the Ouseburn Valley in Newcastle upon Tyne holds a visual record of some of the most innovative techniques in construction and the work of pioneers in engineering.

Those of us involved in nurturing the future development of the Ouseburn Valley are also entrusted with the conservation and preservation of these remarkable structures standing in a cradle of the industrial revolution and illustrating English engineering heritage at its best.

In addition this book hopes to bring this often hidden story to a wider audience.

There will no doubt be further bridges spanning the river and the valley. We hope that the future designers will respect the past pioneers and perhaps bring new innovative techniques to add to those already on display.

Byker Metro Bridge, 2013.
Opposite page: The Cluny Footbridge, 2013.

33

Timeline

Date	English transport historical events	Events in Ouseburn
Pre Roman times		Natural ford crossed the Ouseburn
A.D.43 to A.D. 410	The Romans ruled in Great Britain	
A.D. 120 - A.D. 122		Hadrian ordered the building of the wall from Wallsend to Bowness
Up to 1600s	Most transport was either by sea or horseback although some people were able to travel in covered wagons (if they were rich) Packhorses single or in droves were the main means of transporting large quantities of goods on land. A packhorse could carry approximately 128 kilos of goods evenly spread between its two side bags.	The Ouseburn was mainly farmland and travel across it was by muddy footpaths and wooden bridges. Coalmining started in many parts of the North East including Ouseburn and the need to transport Coal down to ships on the River Tyne was necessary. Packhorse routes developed to bring coal through the Ouseburn from Kenton and Jesmond.
1619		First wooden bridge across the Ouseburn was built on the Quayside Road across to the Glasshouses
1635	In 1635 the Royal Post which carried mail for Charles I around England was allowed to carry letters for people who paid his messengers.	Other pathways across Ouseburn were developed from St. Ann's to Byker Bar and Stepney to Heaton
1663	Turnpike Roads were introduced in 1663 and some developed between most major towns in UK	The Shields Turnpike Route from Newcastle to North Shields commenced from Pilgrim Street in Newcastle.
1669		The old wooden bridge at Glasshouses was replaced with one of stone
1727		The Glasshouse Stone Bridge was made level and 2 years later in 1729 the wooden bridge on the Shields Turnpike route was replaced with a stone structure.
1750s	Many canals were built in England although none in the North East of England as transport was still mainly by packhorse and sailing ships from the navigable rivers.	The bridge known as Crawford's Bridge which crosses the Ouseburn between Stepney and Byker Bar/Heaton was constructed of stone although it probably replaced a wooden structure.
1790	Carts and carriages pulled by horses were introduced.	The bridge on the Shields Turnpike was widened to accommodate wider modes of transport.
1801		James & Co opened their white lead works on the west bank of the Ouseburn and constructed a single-arch stone bridge just west of Crawford's Bridge to allow the transport of goods down river.
1815	Steamships were invented and the first of them to cross the Atlantic sailed in 1838 taking 19 days to reach America.	
1825	Stockton to Darlington Railway opened.	
1837		North Shields Railway Company built a line between Newcastle and North Shields which crossed the Ouseburn with the construction of their laminated wooden viaduct.
1840s	By 1840s most major towns were connected by railway.	

1860	Passengers throughout England began to use public transport in the form of horse-drawn trams.
1869	In 1869 the wooden structure of the railway viaduct was replaced with iron in the same style as the original and the whole bridge widened.
1878	The Glasshouse Bridge was replaced with the brick structure we see today and after 27 years of discussion, Byker Road Bridge is finally opened to pedestrians.
1881	Byker Bridge Company planned widening of the bridge to accommodate new footpaths and tramlines for electric trams.
1885	The Motorbike was patented and also cycling started to become popular
1885-6	Karl Benz made the first motor cars and this mode of transport became popular very quickly leading to the need for better roads
1904	The North Eastern Railway Company electrified the stretch between Newcastle and Tynemouth making this the first stretch of electrified railway in the UK.
1906 - 1911	Ouseburn Culvert was constructed and the land filled in, in order to provide space to build housing but this never materialised.
1908	The old stone Glasshouse Bridge which stood in front of the new bridge was demolished as part of the Quayside improvements. A new bridge carrying a single track railway and a road was constructed using hot-riveting techniques.
1930s	Most towns had the beginnings of a motorised tram service for public transport either on rails or operated with overhead cables.
1940s	1 in 10 families owned a car.
1950s	Motorised trams were gradually replaced with modern day motor buses.
1960s	1 in 3 families owned a car.
1970s	Most families owned at least 1 car.
1972	Derelict land under the Ouseburn Viaduct was tidied and the Ouseburn Culvert was extended to include the Ford & Co bridge.
1982	Ouseburn Metro Bridge was constructed as the new Metro System was build across the city.
2003	The Cluny Footbridge was installed as part of the new Ouseburn Farm building.
2013	The Ouseburn Viaduct was completely renovated and coated with a long-lasting paint product.

Facts and Figures

Hadrian's Wall

English Heritage: Scheduled Monument status under the Ancient Monuments and Archaeological Areas Act 1979. Hadrian's Wall in wall mile 2, Byker section of Hadrian's Wall and presumed site of milecastle 3 at Shields Road West. English Heritage List Number 1003508. UNESCO World Heritage Site: Frontiers of the Roman Empire.

Construction date	A.D. 120 - A.D. 122
Designer/Engineer	Praefectus castronum of each legion was responsible for drawing plans and overseeing work.
Builders	Most probably Legions II Augusta, VI Victrix & XX Valeria Victrix.
Length	118km
Width	8.3 to 8.8 Roman Feet - 1RF = 296mm (Approx. 2.5m)
Height of Wall when in situ	15 Roman Feet high (4.44metres)

Crawford's Bridge

Grade II listed building. First listed on 30th March 1987. English Heritage List Ref. Number 1024785.

Construction date	Before 1750
Designer	Unknown
Engineer	Unknown
Contractor	Unknown
Approximate or exact cost	Unknown
Length	Unknown
Width	Unknown
Height above water level	Unknown

James & Co Bridge

Construction date	1801
Designer	Unknown
Engineer	Unknown
Contractor	Unknown
Approximate or exact cost	Unknown
Length	Unknown
Width	Unknown
Height above water level	Unknown

Ouseburn Railway Viaduct

Grade II* listed building. First listed on 12th Nov 1965. English Heritage List Ref. Number 1120788.

Construction date	13 Jan 1837 - 18 Jun 1839
Designer	
Engineer	John & Benjamin Green
Contractor	Messrs. Welsh
Approximate or exact cost	£24,500
Engineer of renovation	Carillion
Designer of renovation	Cass Hayward
Approximate or exact cost of 2012-13 renovation	£10million
Length	918 feet (279.81m)
Width	50 feet (15.24m)
Height above water level	108.26 feet (32.998 metres)

New Glasshouse Bridge

Construction date	21 May 1878
Designer	Unknown
Engineer	Robert Hodgson and Edmund Forbes
Contractor	Sir Walter Scott
Approximate or exact cost	£14,000
Length	270 feet (82.296m)
Width	25 feet (76.2m)
Height above water level	56 feet (17.07m) low water & 37.6 feet (11.46m) high water

Byker Road Bridge

Construction date	19 October 1878
Designer	John Fulton
Engineer	Robert Hodgson and later

Structure	Construction date	Designer	Engineer	Contractor	Approximate or exact cost	Length	Width	Height above water level
(continued from previous page)					approx. £50,000	1130 feet (344.42metres)	30 Feet (9.144 Metres)	106 feet (32.309m)
Ouseburn Culvert	1907 to 1911	City Engineers	F.J. Edge & later C.R.S. Kirkpatrick (City Engineers)	W.T. Weir	Approx. £160,766 including compulsory purchase although the actual culvert was estimated at £81,463.	2150 feet (655.32m)	30 feet (9.144m)	Tunnel height 20 feet (6.096m)
Low Level Bridge	1908	City Engineers	Unknown	Unknown	Unknown	74 feet 6 inches (22.738 metres)	61 feet (18.593 metres)	Unknown
Ouseburn Bridge	1959	Newcastle City Council Engineers		Unknown	Unknown	37 feet 6 inches (11.43 metres)	51 feet (15.545 metres)	13 feet 7 inches – High Water Mark (4.14 metres) in 1959
Byker Metro Bridge	Jun 1976 to 11 Nov 1982	Ove Arup & Partners		John Mowlem	Cost of whole metro system approx. £284 million before addition of Sunderland extension at £149 million	2674 feet (815.04 metres)	27 feet (8.2296 metres)	98 feet 5 inches (30 metres)
Cluny Footbridge	Spring 2004	Concrete & Timber Services Ltd			Unknown	29 feet 6 inches (9 metres)	9 feet 10 inches (3 metres)	6 feet 6 inches (2 metres)

Bibliography

Barke, M and Buswell, R.J. (editors) Newcastle's changing map, Newcastle upon Tyne City Libraries & Arts, ISBN 0 902653 91 1.

British Newspaper Archives

Charlton, R. J. A history of Newcastle upon Tyne, William H Robinson, 1885.

Conradi, J. F. Types of railway steel bridge floors, The Railway Magazine, 1898, Volume 3, pp 282-287.

Hearnshaw, F.J.C. The story of English Towns Newcastle upon Tyne, The Sheldon Press, 1924.

Hill, Peter The construction of Hadrian's Wall, The History Press, 2006, ISBN 978 0 7524 4011 8.

Hutton, Charles Map of Newcastle 1772.

Jarvis, Adrian Portrait of the Liverpool Overhead Railway, Ian Allan, 1996.

Jervoise, E The ancient bridges of the north of England, The Architectural Press, 1931.

Mackenzie, Eanus A descriptive and historical account of the town and county of Newcastle upon Tyne, Mackenzie & Dent, 1827.

Newcastle City Libraries Tyneside Life and Times on Flickr and hard-copy collection.

Newcastle City Libraries Local Studies Collection.

Newcastle City Council Minutes 1837 - 1960.

Oliver, Thomas A new picture of Newcastle upon Tyne, T. Oliver, 1831.

Rennison, R.W. Three Overlooked Bridges in Newcastle, Archaeologia Aeliana, 5th Series, Volume 30, pp 163 – 172.

Stuckley, William Itinerarium Curiosum Volume II, Baker and Leigh, 1776.

Sykes, John Local Records or Historical Register of remarkable events, Volume 1, T. Fordyce, 1886.

The Engineer Ouseburn Culvert, November 2, 1906 pp 440-441.

Yorke, Trevor Bridges explained viaducts aqueducts, Countryside Books, 2008 ISBN 978 1 84674 079 4.

Weinthal, Leo The story of the Cape to Cairo railway and river route, 1887 – 1922, Pioneer, 1923.

Welford, Richard History of Newcastle and Gateshead, W. Scott, 1884.

Index